LAWS OF SUCCESS MAGNETISM

OLA OBEMBE

Copyright © Ola Obembe
All Rights Reserved.

This book has been published with all efforts taken to make the material error-free after the consent of the author. However, the author and the publisher do not assume and hereby disclaim any liability to any party for any loss, damage, or disruption caused by errors or omissions, whether such errors or omissions result from negligence, accident, or any other cause.

While every effort has been made to avoid any mistake or omission, this publication is being sold on the condition and understanding that neither the author nor the publishers or printers would be liable in any manner to any person by reason of any mistake or omission in this publication or for any action taken or omitted to be taken or advice rendered or accepted on the basis of this work. For any defect in printing or binding the publishers will be liable only to replace the defective copy by another copy of this work then available.

This book is dedicated to all success lover and those who aspires to be successful.

Contents

ONE
PERSONAL MAGNETISM.

Let us understand. You cannot reasonably hope to succeed by merely dreaming about success. You surely cannot achieve success if you plunge blindly through your career. You cannot succeed without possessing some degree of personal magnetism. When you began reading this book, you certainly possessed a measure of magnetic capacity, either physical or psychic. If you have energetically observed its directions, you have developed both varieties; but, above that, you have also combined them into one living whole, the magnetic personality.

This result has required at least a year of persistent effort. If you have arrived at this point in less time, you should go back and begin where haste first retarded your progress.

Magnetism is natural growth.

No matter how great may be your ability to read and understand books, that growth, that law, requires time as well as intelligent effort. No matter how poor may be your ability in such respect, that growth is certain if you put reasonable time and genuine effort into its acquisition.

The giant trees of California were once puny saplings. The slow lapse of time has drawn nature into their mighty hearts. Magnetism can no more be acquired by the mere reading an article, or by the hurried practice of its directions, than can these giants of the West be produced in the hot-house culture of a northern summer.

Magnetic growth is naturally slow. Its principles, its methods, and the results of its study have to be deeply sunk into and absorbed and assimilated by the subjective self before the reaction of magnetism in the objective life can obtain. If you have read these lines correctly, you have learned that magnetic growth cannot be hurried. These statements are placed here because, had they appeared at the beginning of our work, the outlook would have seemed, perhaps, discouraging, but more especially because they would not have been understood. You now understand them because you have toiled, and you can afford to smile at such possible discouragement. You have paid an easy price for magnetic power, for the gains discount the pains.

Magnetism and practical life.

The faithful observance of these suggestions has developed many surprises during the time occupied. The growth of magnetism involves the intense and continuous concentration of thought upon the psychic field, and you may likely find it necessary to guard against that danger. The method of guarding is briefly indicated below.

The sole value of magnetism consists in its practical application to everyday affairs. Success-Magnetism is not an accomplishment merely; it is a practical power. When rightly developed and used, it controls the subjective self in the concrete work of the objective. The definition of the goal you have been seeking now appears:

Success-magnetism is personal magnetism intelligently multiplied into actual life.

The first duty of man is practical sanity.

TWO

19 LAWS OF MAGNETIC DEVELOPMENT.

FIRST LAW: Discovery of the endowment. The limits of magnetic endowment latent in every normal person emerge only through prolonged effort in the culture of magnetism.

SECOND LAW: Difficult environment. Magnetism develops in direct proportion to the difficulty of the environment.

THIRD LAW: Magnetic intention. Magnetism evolves solely through the multiplication of endowment into the environment by the persistent magnetic intention.

FOURTH LAW: Free adjustment. The culture of magnetism imperatively demands that central adjustment of the self to all powers which realizes absolute psychic freedom.

FIFTH LAW: Concentration. The magnetic multiplication of endowment into the environment is only possible to intense, persistent, and unified concentration to the methods of Success-Magnetism.

SIXTH LAW: Purpose-ideals. Growth of noblest magnetism depends, in the larger sense, upon general adherence to a single, preeminent, ideal life purpose, and, in the particular sense, upon specialization of the individual in studied magnetic conduct related to that end.

SEVENTH LAW: Receptivity. The highest magnetism realizes through magnetic laws in proportion as the inner self maintains alert receptivity to the Universal Forces.

EIGHTH LAW: Demand. The silent, persistent demand of the self upon the Universal Magnetism makes it a center toward which the Forces naturally gravitate.

NINTH LAW: Affirmation. Continuous, intense affirmation of actual possessed magnetic power stimulates the success elements, maintains receptivity, emphasizes demand, harmonizes and intensifies inner etheric vibrations, and induces a positive movement of the universal ether and its forces inward toward the central self.

TENTH LAW: Psychic energy. All personal magnetism involves psychic energy developed and directed by magnetic intention.

ELEVENTH LAW: Self-control. Magnetic energy concentrates through psychic control of its tendencies.

TWELFTH LAW: Magnetic quality. The inner psychic attitude the character of magnetic intention determines the quality and effectiveness of the effort to multiply endowment into the environment, and, therefore, the kind and degree of magnetism attained.

THIRTEENTH LAW: Self-valuation. Other things being equal, magnetism unfolds as gratifying but unostentatious, self-valuation develops.

FOURTEENTH LAW: Use of self. Under conformity to other magnetic laws, the highest magnetism issues only from the constant best use of self at its best to the best advantage.

FIFTEENTH LAW: Magnetic heroism. Self-pity, complaint, and all kindred states confuse, weaken and waste every variety of magnetic power, while heroic acceptance of conditions for their betterment, and courageous assertion of self as master, conserve, and enormously develop the noblest magnetism in proportion to the sway of the magnetic intention.

SIXTEENTH LAW: Action and reaction. Highest magnetism involves not only studied cultivation but, as well, the magnetic utilization of stimulating reactions induced by intelligent employment.

SEVENTEENTH LAW: Recovery. Whoever, on the occasion of any psychic (magnetic) failure or defeat, dedicates the whole of aroused desperation to the recovery of ground, infallibly induces a stress in the etheric life around him which ultimately draws to his aid, with the onsweep of worlds, the Universal Forces.

EIGHTEENTH LAW: Reproduction. "Everything is transmitted, everything is transformed, everything is reproduced" (Ochorowicz); in physical and psychic health alone, therefore, are the Universal Forces transmitted through perfect etheric vibrations, transformed through effective etheric conduction, and reproduced in magnetism by adequate and harmonious psychic control of etheric capabilities.

NINETEENTH LAW: Superiority of culture. The crude values of natural magnetism, the automatic functions of unconscious magnetism, demonstrate at their best solely as they climax in full conscious magnetic culture.

THREE

31 LAWS OF MAGNETIC ACTION.

FIRST LAW: Relation of Power to "Tone". The effectiveness of magnetism in action depends upon harmony of "tone" between its possessor and any other person, and in securing such "tone" harmony, on any magnetic plane, in any particular psychic state, at any given time, psychic and physical magnetism mutually cooperate.

SECOND LAW: Magnetic Intention. The magnetic intention ("I INTEND MAGNETICALLY") intensifies otherwise unconscious magnetism, and runs through all the mass of general etheric vibrations like a theme in complicated music, imparting to them unity, character, intelligence, and definite and enormous effectiveness in practical employment.

THIRD LAW: Influence of Purpose. In the employment of magnetism, long-run purpose establishes etheric character, and specialized purpose confirms that character if it concentrates the general purpose, but confuses that character, perhaps destroys it, if it antagonizes the general purpose.

FOURTH LAW: Force of the Ideal. The idealism of motive determines the character of etheric vibrations, and the idealism of magnetic activities determines the quality of magnetism achieved.

FIFTH LAW: Sway of Other Interest. The general sway of other interest in life, and the particular influence of other interest on special occasions, impart to uses of magnetism enormous effectiveness, and not least concerning the self.

SIXTH LAW: Reaction of Admiration. The consciousness of admiration for others, recognized by them, reacts with tremendous power to stimulate magnetic action.

SEVENTH LAW: Measure of the Intake. In the magnetic life, intake of power is correctly measured by the output of power: inversely in waste, directly in intelligent expenditure.

EIGHTH LAW: Adjustment. Magnetic effectiveness is proportioned to accuracy and fulness of adjustment, to things, to laws, to forces, to times, to situations, to qualities, to facts, to truths, to persons, and only studied experience can discover and establish such adjustment.

The problems of adjustment to persons are these:

With inferiors, to put self magnetically,

without the appearance of condescension,

on their levels for the end in view, applying then the general principles of magnetism.

With equals, to apply the general principles.

With superiors, to assume their level while magnetically deferring, without adulation or humility, to such superiority, regardless of its reality or unreality, for the end in view, applying the general principles of magnetism.

NINTH LAW: The magnetism of identity. The magnetic value of adjustment expresses the force and completeness with which the individual can identify himself with another person, suggesting oneness through attitude, gesture, act, eye, tone, language, and telepathic sympathy.

TENTH LAW: The use of reactions. Magnetic skill exhibits in the manner in which beneficial reactions are received and utilized, negative or indifferent reactions are ostensibly ignored, yet constituted stimulation for further persistent magnetic action, and hostile reactions are refused, without ostentation, but with determination (if worthwhile) to "win out" through better adjustment and increased magnetic endeavor.

ELEVENTH LAW: Magnetic attack. Magnetic success demands the direct attack when etheric harmony of "tone" is assured, but the indirect method otherwise; that is, such attack methods as will secure that harmony.

TWELFTH LAW: The conquest of antagonism. Magnetism ostensibly ignored, and refrains from, exciting antagonism; but, when antagonism is evident, rejects it and proceeds on the indirect attack, or openly accepts it and adopts the direct or the indirect method as the one or the other promises speediest and most perfect harmony of "tone".

THIRTEENTH LAW: Mortal antipathies. Success-Magnetism conquers the influence of deep-seated natural antipathies only by avoiding their causes.

FOURTEENTH LAW: Re-adjustment. The etheric life is an unceasing reaction, and magnetism, therefore, demonstrates itself by squaring with every issue and making every change and every defeat a new opportunity.

FIFTEENTH LAW: Control of output. It is important to know when to open the circuit that is, to cut off the current of magnetic force as it is to know when to close the circuit to pour forth magnetic influences.

SIXTEENTH LAW: Concession. Concession becomes magnetic in its timeliness. If premature or belated, it defeats magnetism.

SEVENTEENTH LAW: Harmonic conditions. Magnetism enhances through the beauty of personal surroundings, cleanliness, order, adornment, art, literature, music, and the like.

EIGHTEENTH LAW: Sovereignty of will. is the director of native and unconscious magnetism and the creator and director of developed magnetism. Power of will is indispensable to magnetic power.

NINETEENTH LAW: Energy in magnetic action. The projection of magnetic influence proportions to the inner, conscious intensity of psychic and nervous states. Exploding powder in the gun calls for the man behind the weapon, the soul within the man, powerful vibrations within the soul's arena, magnetic intention within the vibrations, and psychic energy within the intention.

TWENTIETH LAW: Self-control. Magnetic power becomes effective precisely as mastery of self, in restraint and handling, approaches perfection.

TWENTY-FIRST LAW: Magnetic handling of self. The attitude of magnetism, the magnetic intention, and psychic pose, "I stand positively magnetic toward this person or this situation," constantly maintained, ultimately instructs in all the arts of magnetic self-handling through the law of auto-suggestion, and realizes in the practical form its ideals.

TWENTY-SECOND LAW: The magnetic mask. The mask of magnetism achieves effectiveness when it covers personal states and purposes in a manner positively to attract, and in that manner alone.

TWENTY-THIRD LAW: Magnetic consciousness. Intense magnetic consciousness without thought concerning it secures, by its uplifting and stimulating influence, the greatest exaltation of personal powers when employed.

TWENTY-FOURTH LAW: Magnetic faith. Deep and vital faith in the certainty of magnetic success renders all latent and developed magnetism dynamic if that faith is thrown into action.

TWENTY-FIFTH LAW: The demand in use. In the application of magnetism to any task, intense, persistent demand upon the Universal Forces swings them directly into the effort.

TWENTY-SIXTH LAW: The affirmation in use. When, in the application of magnetism, one affirms, mentally, intensely, persistently, "I am receiving and exerting power," he unconsciously calls to aid all the success elements and makes himself a center toward which the Universal Forces inevitably gravitate.

TWENTY-SEVENTH LAW: The magnetic telescope. The magnetic attitudes, faith, demand, and affirmation, constitute a magnetic telescope through which the distant goal of success is magnified and all nearer obstacles, lures, and irritating conditions are closed out of view.

TWENTY-EIGHTH LAW: Magnetic accumulations. Magnetism, through correct application to life, not only develops in the individual, but accumulates in his environment, and reacts beneficially without direct personal supervision.

TWENTY-NINTH LAW: The personal atmosphere. The personal atmosphere exactly reflects the inner self, and it furnishes a perfect field for magnetic effectiveness only when the self and the body are clean and buoyantly healthy.

THIRTIETH LAW: Subordination of physical magnetism. In the subordination of physical to psychic magnetism, each finds its greatest effectiveness according to the relative development of both orders.

THIRTY-FIRST LAW: The fixed idea. Long-continued association with some fixed, great and attractive idea sets into operation certain deep, subconscious operations of the soul, which, for a time unrecognized and unmanifest in life, gradually and surely coordinate all individual powers thereto, induce a working of the whole system in harmony therewith, and finally emerge in the objective life and consciousness as a unified, actual dynamic force.

The idea has swung the individual, has transformed him, has harmonized and intensified his faculties and his ether, has come to sovereignty in his atmosphere, and from there exerts a dynamic force upon other people and life's conditions.

This book has tried to saturate you with the idea of success coordinating with its necessary elements and has thus endeavored to swing your whole being into a mighty belief that large success is also for you.